P9-DGW-403

A Tribute to
THE YOUNG AT HEART

A.A. MILNE

By Jill C. Wheeler

Published by Abdo & Daughters, 6535 Cecilia Circle, Edina, Minnesota 55439.

Library bound edition distributed by Rockbottom Books, Pentagon Tower, P.O. Box 36036, Minneapolis, Minnesota 55435.

Printed in the United States.

Cover Photo: UPI / Bettmann
Inside Photos: UPI / Bettmann 5,15, 20, 22 & 25
                 FPG 13 & 16

Edited by Rosemary Wallner

LIBRARY OF CONGRESS CATALOGING-IN-PUBLICATION DATA

Wheeler, Jill C., 1964-
    A.A. Milne : creator of Winnie the Pooh / written by Jill C. Wheeler; [edited by Rosemary Wallner].
        p. cm. -- (The Young at Heart)
    Summary: Discusses the life and works of the Englishman who wrote thousands of articles, plays, stories, and novels, yet is best remembered for his creation, Winnie the Pooh.
    ISBN 1-56239-114-3 (lib. bdg.)
    1. Milne, A.A. (Alan Alexander), 1882-1956 -- Juvenile literature. 2. Authors, English -- 20th century -- Biography -- Juvenile literature. 3. Children's stories, English -- History and criticism -- Juvenile literature. 4. Winnie-the-Pooh (Fictitious character) -- Juvenile literature. [1. Milne, A.A. (Alan Alexander), 1882-1956. 2. Authors, English.] I. Wallner, Rosemary, 1964- . II. Title. III. Series: Wheeler, Jill C., 1964- Young at Heart.
PR6025.I65Z97 1992   828'.91209--dc20   92-16570
                                              [B]

International Standard Book Number:	Library of Congress Catalog Card Number:
1-56239-114-3	92-16570

TABLE OF CONTENTS

OF BEARS, PIGLETS AND A HUNDRED ACRE WOOD

Millions of adults and children received a special treat in 1966. That year, filmmaker Walt Disney brought Winnie-the-Pooh and his friends to movie theaters. The Disney studios called the movie *Winnie-the-Pooh and The Honey Tree.*

The movie delighted audiences of all ages. Everyone laughed at the silly old bear who loved honey so much he got stuck in a tree. Some children had never seen the world's most famous bear before then. Many adults remembered reading Winnie-the-Pooh stories when they were young.

The movie created new interest in Pooh and his friends. People wanted to see more of Pooh, Piglet, Eeyore, Rabbit and Owl. They wanted to romp through the Hundred Acre Wood, too. Many bought the books *Winnie-the-Pooh* and *The House at Pooh Corner* for the first time.

Walt Disney's first Pooh movie came out forty years after *Winnie-the-Pooh* first arrived in book stores. By that time, the Pooh books had been translated into 25 languages.

A. A. Milne,"The King of the Children's Book World."

Readers around the world had bought more than seven million copies of the books. The man who created the honey-loving bear had become a celebrity. He was an Englishman named Alan Alexander Milne. He wrote under the name A.A. Milne.

Milne wrote many things during his life, including plays, articles, short stories and novels. His writings brought joy and laughter to millions of people. A reviewer once commented on Milne's lighthearted style. "The dominant note in everything he has written, for mature people or little folk," the critic said, "is a joy in all life."

I CAN DO IT!

One summer day in 1884, John Milne decided it was time his two oldest sons learned to read. David was nearly five years old and Kenneth almost four. John put a chart of words on the wall. When he left the room, David and Kenneth were staring silently at the chart. Their brother, Alan, was playing in the corner.

When John returned, he pointed to a word on the chart. "What's that?" he asked. The two older boys remained silent. Then, from the back of the room he heard Alan. "I can do it," two-and-a-half-year-old Alan said. "What's that?" John asked again, amazed. "Cat," Alan replied with a grin. The boy was right.

It was no surprise Alan Alexander Milne learned to read and write early. He was born on January 18, 1882, to teachers John and Maria Milne. Milne and his family grew up in Henley House, the London school his father operated. Milne could hardly wait until he could go to classes at Henley House, too.

He got his chance in September 1888 when he was just six years old. Milne was among the youngest students at Henley House. He also was different from many other children in that he enjoyed school as much as he enjoyed playing games. He earned higher marks than other boys his age. A school report on Milne praised his work. It said Milne could "speak 556 words per minute and write more in three minutes than his instructor can read in thirty."

Milne began writing at an early age. He wrote stories about football games and long walks. The Henley House School magazine published some of his stories. It helped that Milne's father was the editor of the magazine.

Henley House had another famous resident, too. A man named H.G. Wells became a science teacher there in 1889. Wells and Milne became good friends. Wells went on to become a famous science fiction writer.

BOARDING SCHOOL DAYS

When Milne was young, many English boys finished their schooling away from home. The schools they attended were called boarding schools. Milne decided he wanted to attend Westminster School after he finished at Henley House. Westminster was a well-known boarding school. He wanted to study mathematics.

Milne's family did not have enough money to pay his tuition at Westminster. He knew he had to get a scholarship if he wanted to go there. He began studying extra hard.

Along with mathematics, he studied Greek and Latin like many other boys his age were doing.

Milne's work paid off. He became the youngest student to earn a scholarship to Westminster School. He began school there when he was just eleven years old. Most boys began at Westminster when they were fourteen.

Milne was a good student. Then a teacher told Milne's father he was doing poorly in mathematics. Actually, Milne was at the head of his class. But John Milne believed the teacher. Milne decided there was no point in working hard at mathematics anymore. He turned his attention to other subjects – including literature.

Milne attended Westminster for seven years. During that time he spent many hours at the library. He enjoyed reading classic tales by Charles Dickens and Jane Austen. He took part in school plays and discovered a love of theater.

However, he still didn't know what he would do for a living once he graduated. His brothers had learned trades and now worked for the government.

Milne knew his father expected him to do the same. Milne thought it would be boring to do such a job. He wanted something more, but he wasn't sure what it was.

Then one day he found a copy of the magazine produced by students at Cambridge University. It was called *The Granta*. Milne made up his mind to attend Cambridge and become the editor of the magazine. He knew his family could not afford to send him to the university. Few people went to college in those days because it cost so much. But he had faced a similar situation to get into Westminster, and he knew what he had to do.

CAMBRIDGE

Once again, Milne won a scholarship so he could make his dream come true. He enrolled at Cambridge in the fall of 1900. He began submitting poems to *The Granta* almost immediately.

The editors at *Granta* rejected most of Milne's poems. They told him he might learn to write if he kept trying. Milne refused to be discouraged and kept on sending in his work.

Finally, in February 1901, one of the his poems appeared in the pages of *The Granta*.

Over the next few years, Milne often wrote for *The Granta*. He also kept up his interest in theater. He joined a Cambridge group called the Trinity College Shakespeare Society. He spent time with the school's debating group and the football team as well. He enjoyed his many activities, but it was always writing that captured his heart.

Then in 1902, the incredible happened. The publishers of *The Granta* asked him to be the new editor. "This was almost the biggest surprise of my life," Milne recalled.

Milne gladly took the editor's job. He encouraged other students to send in their work while he continued to submit his. Under his eye, the magazine improved. More and more people read it. Now more than ever before, Milne's heart belonged to journalism.

Milne finished at Cambridge in the summer of 1903. His father still wanted him to work for the government or to be a teacher. Milne still thought those jobs would be boring. Finally, he told his father he wanted to be a writer.

He wrote a letter to his friend H.G. Wells telling of his decision. "I am going to try my luck at journalism," he wrote. "Thanks to an arrangement with my father... I have enough money to keep me somehow in London for two years – even if I earn nothing. But I'm going to earn something. You see!"

STRUGGLING FREELANCER

London had many newspapers and magazines in 1903. The city also had many journalists who wanted their work printed in those publications. People who write for a variety of publications are called freelance writers. Milne became a freelance writer, too. He had many articles rejected. Even when a publication bought one of his articles, he received only a little money.

More than anything, Milne wanted to get published in *Punch*. *Punch* was one of England's most popular magazines at that time. Unlike many other magazines, it printed many humorous columns and cartoons. Milne began writing columns especially to send to *Punch*. Time after time the editors rejected his work. Finally, in 1905, *Punch* began buying many of his articles.

H. G. Wells was a good friend of A. A. Milne.

Milne loved having his work appear in *Punch*, but the magazine did not pay him much money. His father's money was nearly gone by now, and he knew he had to do something different. He told the editor at *Punch* he would not write anymore magazine articles. He said he planned to write a novel instead. He thought he could make more money that way.

He was surprised when the *Punch* editor contacted him. The editor said the magazine wanted to hire him as associate editor. Milne could not believe his good luck. Another of his dreams came true in February 1906, when he joined the *Punch* staff. Now his work would appear in the magazine every week.

After four years with *Punch*, Milne had written many articles and developed many fans. He collected his *Punch* articles and published them in a book called *The Day's Play*. That same year, he met the *Punch* editor's goddaughter. Her name was Dorothy de Selincourt. She asked him to call her Daphne. In the summer of 1913, they were married.

A. A. Milne with his wife Daphne.

H. G. Wells (right) on the French Front during WWI.

A WRITER GOES TO WAR

Life continued happily for Milne. He was earning a reputation in literary circles for his work with *Punch*. He had a new wife and a new house. In 1914, Milne published his second book of articles. That same year, World War I began. Milne would have been very happy had it not been for the war.

Milne hated war more than anything else. "War is the most babyish and laughably idiotic thing that this world has evolved," he said. He did not believe people should settle their differences by fighting. He watched as many of his friends and family went off to fight. He did not want to go. But in early 1915, he volunteered to fight for England.

The Army sent Milne to the Isle of Wight to help train soldiers. The Isle of Wight is a part of England. Daphne joined him there. In the evenings, Milne would dictate stories to her while she wrote them down. Together, they turned the stories into a play. Milne was ready to bring the play to the stage when the Army sent him to France in July 1916.

Milne's military career took a turn for the worse. He became a soldier in the muddy trenches and battlefields of France. He saw hundreds of men killed, including some of his good friends. Though he remained on the staff of *Punch*, he could not write humorous articles. He couldn't find much to laugh about in the middle of so much death and destruction.

In November 1916, Milne became very ill. He had a temperature of 105 degrees. The Army sent him back to England. When he recovered, he and Daphne returned to the Isle of Wight and Milne instructed soldiers once again. He was grateful to be alive, but the war had changed him. He vowed to show people war was not the answer.

SUCCESSFUL PLAYWRIGHT

Milne began to write plays during the war. "My job was soldiering and my spare time was my own affair," he said. "Others played bridge and golf. That was one way of amusing oneself. Another way was to write plays."

Milne's first play was produced on a London stage in April 1917. The actors and actresses performed the play one day after the United States entered World War I.

Milne still had not recovered fully from his illness. He asked the Army for a less strenuous job and they put him to work writing for the Army in London. He worked at the War Office during the day and wrote at night. Soon his plays – not his *Punch* articles – were the works that got him noticed. Some actors and actresses even asked him to write plays just for them.

His most famous play took to the stage in 1920. He called it *Mr. Pim Passes By.* Later that year, Milne and Daphne had a son. They named him Christopher Robin. For his first birthday, they gave him a stuffed bear. It grew to be his favorite toy.

In 1921, Milne tried his hand at writing novels. Many people enjoyed his book *The Red House Mystery.* It proved Milne could write serious mysteries as well as funny plays and articles. His plays continued to be popular, too. Once five of his plays were running at the same time.

A. A. Milne. Once five of his plays were running at the same time.

WHEN WE WERE VERY YOUNG

In 1923, the editor of a new children's magazine asked Milne to write a poem for her publication. He put aside a detective novel he was writing to work on the poem. He thought it would be a new challenge to write for children. He also wanted to write something different since he felt children's literature was too full of baby talk.

Milne had plenty of inspiration for his poem. He liked to watch his young son, Christopher Robin. Christopher Robin's funny ways always made him think of poems. He enjoyed watching his son splash around in puddles or drag his teddy bear behind him down the stairs. He wrote several children's poems and even put Christopher Robin's name in some.

Milne selected one of his children's poems to send to the magazine. Then he decided to write a whole book of poems for children. He finished the book in just a few weeks and sent the poems to his publisher.

Christopher Robin and his father at their home in England.

The publisher liked the poems and asked a man named Edward Shepard to illustrate the book. Shepard and Milne ended up working together for many years. Some people still think of Shepard's drawings when they think of Winnie-the-Pooh.

Milne's publisher printed the book of poems in 1924 under the title, *When We Were Very Young* . The book was an instant success. It sold thousands of copies in Europe and in the United States. People wanted to know more about Christopher Robin. In England, people recognized the real Christopher Robin on the street.

HELLO, POOH

Christopher Robin did not mind his new fame. He was content to stay home and play with his stuffed animals. Among them was a roly-poly bear he called Pooh. He named it after a swan he saw that people called Pooh. Christopher Robin and the bear often had imaginary conversations. Milne and Daphne loved to listen to what Christopher Robin and Pooh were talking about.

Milne noticed his son's love for his teddy bear. He even made up a special bedtime story for Christopher Robin. It was a story about a chubby bear, a balloon and some bees.

The bear's arms were too short to reach its nose, so it had to blow as hard as it could when the bees landed on its nose.

In 1925, the editors of the *Evening News* asked Milne to write a special children's story for their Christmas edition. At first, Milne did not know what to write. Then Daphne suggested he write one of the bedtime stories he told Christopher Robin. Milne quickly wrote down the story he had created about the chubby bear. He named the bear Winnie-the-Pooh.

The story was so successful Milne decided to write a book of stories about Winnie-the-Pooh. He added other characters from Christopher Robin's nursery – a donkey named Eeyore and a pig named Piglet. He made up the characters of Owl and Rabbit. He and Daphne went to a store and bought Kanga and Roo. He set his stories in a place called the Hundred Acre Wood. He modeled it after a real place called Ashdown Forest.

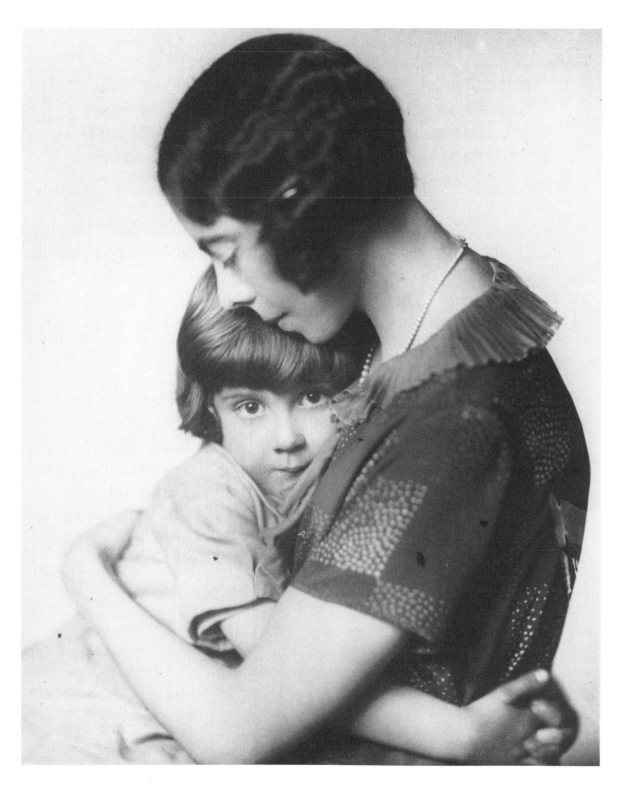

Mrs. A. A. Milne and son Christopher Robin in 1926.

Milne finished his stories in March 1926. He invited Edward Shepard to visit Christopher Robin's nursery and see the animals so he could draw them. Milne's American publisher, John Macrae, remembers seeing the two work together.

Macrae said he remembered watching "Milne sitting on the sofa reading the story. Christopher Robin was sitting on the floor playing with the characters. By his side...sat E.H. Shepard making sketches for illustrations... . Christopher Robin...was entirely unconscious of his part in the drama."

Winnie-the-Pooh hit the book stores in October 1926. Critics loved the book, as did readers. The book sold 150,000 copies in the United States alone by the end of the year. Some people joked that adults liked the book even more than children did.

LOSING A BROTHER

Milne was delighted at the success of *Winnie-the-Pooh*. He began writing more Pooh stories. He also wrote another book of children's verse called *Now We Are Six*. *Now We Are Six* featured the characters from *Winnie-the-Pooh*, too. Meanwhile, he wrote more plays. People began to notice him more for his children's books than for his plays.

In 1928, Milne published a second book of Pooh stories called *The House at Pooh Corner*. The book introduced a bouncy tiger named Tigger. Like his earlier children's books, *The House at Pooh Corner* was a hit. Milne couldn't be completely happy, however. He learned his brother Kenneth was very ill.

Kenneth died in May 1929. Milne felt a part of his childhood had died along with him. Many of Milne's stories came from happy childhood memories. Now those memories were painful. He could not bring himself to write for children again.

BACK TO THE STAGE

Milne returned to writing plays and novels. In 1930, his play *Toad of Toad Hall* was performed for the first time in London. Milne had been working on the play since 1921. The play's characters Rat, Toad, Mole and Badger became favorites of many children. Critics said the play was similar to the Pooh stories. *Toad of Toad Hall* is the only Milne play regularly performed today.

Milne also had the chance to spend more time with his son. He was not as busy as he had been before.

Christopher Robin was in boarding school by that time. During the holidays, the boy was glad to come home and spend time with his father. The two became closer than ever.

In 1931, the Milnes visited America to promote Milne's new novel, *Two People*. They also saw the opening of one of his plays on Broadway.

Milne was surprised so many Americans recognized his name. They usually linked him with Winnie-the-Pooh.

He found it did not matter that he was promoting his latest book. "I always like my last book best," Milne said. "But I find it's impossible to get away from the Christopher Robin atmosphere."

A PLEA FOR PEACE

In the next five years, Milne published six books. He called one *Peace with Honour*. It was a serious book that told of Milne's feelings on war. He urged readers to avoid war at all costs. He felt it was his best book yet.

Around the same time, Milne tried an experiment. He had not sent any writing to *Punch* for many years. He asked a friend to sign a manuscript he wrote, and then he sent the article to *Punch*. The editors of *Punch* rejected the article thinking it was from an unknown writer. Milne sent the same article to them again. This time he signed it "A.A. Milne" and *Punch* accepted it.

Four years later, war broke out again. The cruelty of German leader Adolf Hitler shocked Milne and millions of other people.

Milne soon changed his mind about war, deciding there were times when it was necessary. He began writing essays urging England to win the war quickly. Some people said his new thoughts on war did not make sense. They reminded him what he had said in *Peace With Honour.*

Milne answered his critics. "I believe that Hitlerism must be killed before war can be killed," he wrote. "In 1933 when I began *Peace with Honour* my only hope of ending war was to publish my views and hope they would have time to spread before war broke out. They did not... . One must hope to be alive to try again after England's victory... ."

The war became even more real for the Milnes in 1940. They left London for their country home. Soon after, London was pounded by German bombs for months on end. Christopher Robin joined the Royal Engineers and left for the Middle East.

The Royal Engineers were a part of England's Army. Christopher Robin went on to Africa and Italy, and finally returned home in 1946. Milne was grateful to have his son back alive. Yet he sensed a distance that had not been there before.

FINAL CHAPTER

Milne published his last book in 1952. *Year In, Year Out* was a collection of essays on many different themes. Sadly, he suffered a stroke soon after the book was published and spent the last three years of his life as an invalid. People around the world mourned when Milne died on January 31, 1956.

Like many writers, Milne hoped people would remember his work. He wrote thousands of articles, plays, stories and novels. He wrote to urge peace and understanding. He wrote to make people laugh and forget their cares. He wrote to remind everyone what it's like to be young.

Many of Milne's writings now are hidden on dusty library shelves. Some have disappeared altogether. But his tales of a "silly old bear" are as popular today as in 1926. Even before he died, Milne knew Winnie-the-Pooh would outlast everything else. He even wrote a poem about that fact:

"If a writer, why not write
On whatever comes in sight?
So – the Children's Books: a short
Intermezzo of a sort;
When I wrote them, little thinking
All my years of pen and inking
Would be almost lost among
Those four trifles for the young."